I'm Peter Parker, a typical teen from the big city. But I'm also Spider-Man, the lovable web-shooting, crime-fighting Super Hero. It can be pretty tricky keeping track of time between school, friends, homework, and hero stuff. Follow me through a typical day and see how I handle some sticky situations along the way.

Like most kids, my day starts with school. Today I miss the bus—again! I dash through the neighborhood to get to my high school on time. I'm pretty fast, so I beat the bus there. The day is off to a good start!

It is eight o'clock.
It's time for Peter to go to school.
Move the hands on the clock to show 8:00.

What time do you go to school?
Move the hands on the clock to show that time.

It's time for science class with my friends Miles and Gwen. Nobody else knows it, but the three of us all have spider-powers! I guess that makes all of us just a little more interested in our science lab.

It is eleven o'clock.
It's time for Peter's favorite class.
Move the hands on the clock to show 11:00.

What time is your favorite class?
Move the hands on the clock to show that time.

Lunchtime! Over tacos and burgers, Miles tells us that there's a villain on the loose in the city. He says we may soon be tangled up with a vile monster named Venom. What time is it? It's time to build up our appetite for crime fighting!

It is twelve o'clock.
It's time for lunch!
Move the hands on the clock to show 12:00.

What time do you have lunch?
Move the hands on the clock to show that time.

Usually we do regular kid stuff after school, but since Venom is on the loose, today we have to deal with him. He's got sharp ugly teeth, mean eyes, and a long, disgusting tongue. He's a really bad guy. What time is it now? It's time to change clothes and get a serious spider grip on the situation.

It is two o'clock.
It's time for Peter to meet his friends.
Move the hands on the clock to show 2:00.

What time do you get together with friends?
Move the hands on the clock to show that time.

At this time of day, some kids are at soccer practice or doing homework. My friends and I have other work to do. Ghost-Spider Gwen and Spider-Man Miles help me keep that vile Venom in sight. The longer he's on the loose, the stronger he gets.

WE SMELLED YOUR MONSTER BREATH A MILE AWAY, VENOM!

It is three o'clock.
It's time for Peter to become Spider-Man.
Move the hands on the clock to show 3:00.

What time do you do your homework?
Move the hands on the clock to show that time.

Now it's time to tie up this whole situation—in a web, that is! We swing up to a rooftop to keep Venom away from our city. On days like today I'm glad to have spider-pals to help me with crime fighting!

It is four o'clock.
It's time for Spider-Man and friends to defeat Venom.
Move the hands on the clock to show 4:00.

What time do you do something heroic?
Move the hands on the clock to show that time.

What time is it now? It's time to swing around the neighborhood and make sure everything is safe. When a villain is on the loose, there's often another one close behind.

It is five o'clock.
It's time for Spidey to explore his neighborhood.
Move the hands on the clock to show 5:00.

What time do you explore your neighborhood?
Move the hands on the clock to show that time.

Sure enough, I spot Green Goblin from a rooftop. I shoot a few webs to stop his flying contraption, and then I tie him up quickly. It's the end of a busy day, so I'm in no mood to play around.

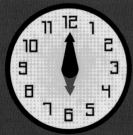

It is six o'clock.
It's time to get the villains off the streets.
Move the hands on the clock to show 6:00.

What time do you clean up?
Move the hands on the clock to show that time.

It's finally dinnertime! Aunt May is cooking up some chili tonight. I take the fastest route possible to get home. After a long day, I don't want to miss a bite. My hunger always reminds me what time it is!

It is seven o'clock.
It's time for dinner at Aunt May's house.
Move the hands on the clock to show 7:00.

What time do you have dinner?
Move the hands on the clock to show that time.

What time is it now? Time for chores. Today's laundry pile could be a tougher job than defeating Venom and the Green Goblin! I tackle it the best I can and start working on my homework.

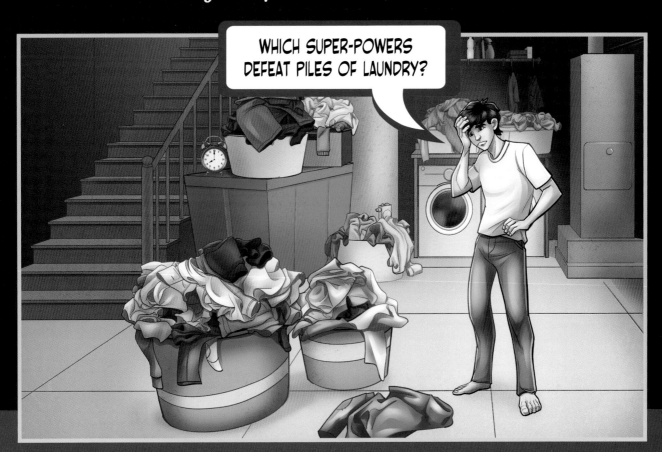

WHICH SUPER-POWERS DEFEAT PILES OF LAUNDRY?

It is eight o'clock.
It's time for Peter to do laundry.
Move the hands on the clock to show 8:00.

What time do you do chores at home?
Move the hands on the clock to show that time.

What a day! After practicing a few new spider-tricks that Miles taught me, I think it's time for bed. Tomorrow will be another action-packed day of school, chores, and hero stuff. I need some sleep!

It is nine o'clock.
It's time for Peter to go to bed.
Move the hands on the clock to show 9:00.

What time do you go to bed?
Move the hands on the clock to show that time.